GIVE MY LOVE TO …

GIVE MY LOVE TO …

Childhood Memories of Evacuation and Wartime London, 1939-45

GRAHAM INWARD

APEX PUBLISHING LTD

First published in 2007 by
Apex Publishing Ltd
PO Box 7086, Clacton on Sea, Essex, CO15 5WN, England

www.apexpublishing.co.uk

British Library Cataloguing-in-Publication Data
A catalogue record for this book
is available from the British Library

ISBN 1-904444-75-X 978-1-904444-75-6

Typeset in 12.5pt Times New Roman
Production Manager: Chris Cowlin
Cover Design: Mark Barnard
Printed and bound in Great Britain

Authors Notes:

Every effort has been made to obtain relevant copyright permission but if anything has inadvertently been overlooked please accept my apologies and this will be dealt with on future re-prints of this book.

I wish to apologise for any offence that may be caused by the use of my cat's name in the letters at the back of this book. Whilst I held my cat in great affection, I was not responsible for giving him a name which was commonly assigned to black animals at that time. I acknowledge, with regret, that the name reflects the lack of awareness in this country in the mid-20th century of the hurt that the use of such a term might engender today.

Dedicated to my dear wife, Annette.

CONTENTS

FOREWORD

Anyone who has lived through the last war, of whatever age, will have memories that will stay with them forever, and according to the circumstances and horror of the event some of those memories will be so intense and disturbing they will never be forgotten and only recalled with much emotional difficulty.

I was a young teenager during the war. My parents were in London, where my Father was a Doctor in general practice, and I was with them for a time before I left for Glasgow to begin an engineering apprenticeship. I experienced at different times the London blitz, the Clydeside blitz and latterly the whole of the VI and V2 rocket attacks, which for some, especially those who survived the whole of the London blitz, were the worst and most unsettling period of aerial bombardment of defenceless citizens, so I have personal experience of a great deal of what the author is writing about.

This modest and delightful little book recaptures some of the emotional responses of a very young boy who lived through the whole period of the last war, sometimes as an evacuee, and some of the time in London. It is a time no one will forget if they are old enough, and I think it is valuable that today's generation, brought up in the welfare state and with so much potential luxury available should know what their parents and grandparents went through in order for them to enjoy the quality of life that most people can experience today.

This moving account of one small boy's experiences during those years between 1939 and 1945 is a valuable addition to the collective memory of a nation.

Nicholas Parsons

INTRODUCTION

VAGUE MEMORIES OF EVACUATION

I was only three years old when war broke out in September 1939 and evacuation from my home in north London (Harringay) began for me at the onset.

Hundreds of isolated memories of evacuation can be recalled, but time permits me to record just some of these. In most cases, I could not put them in a systematic order, not knowing whether some events took place early or late in the war, particularly those concerned with one house, Thorn Cottage, where I had three separate stays in five years. I was greatly helped by the discovery, amongst my late father's private papers, of a bundle of 36 letters, most of which are correspondence between me and my father during my evacuation, and my first school reports. These did not significantly add to my memories, but they did enable me to put many into an approximate sequence which greatly aided my mental picture of evacuation.

Also, reading my letters gave me a clearer understanding of my own feelings. It was interesting to note what was important to me and how I kept referring to home and all it involved, and wanting parts of it in the form of toys. I also consulted my mother, who was with me for most of my evacuation, but I did not want her to add too much information as this might distort my own memories.

I have, therefore, deduced that my evacuation took the following four stages. In between most stages I returned to London.

1. Outbreak of war until early 1940. To Wisbech (one house) and Cambridge (two houses) under the Government Evacuation Scheme for mothers and preschool children (all Hornsey schools were also evacuated to Wisbech). This was an unhappy time for my mother, but I have no significant memories of this period.

2a. Thorn Cottage, in Alton (Hampshire). First stay, autumn 1940 (the London Blitz) and for most (or all) of 1941, with my mother.

2b. YWCA (Young Women's Christian association) Alton, early 1942 until December 1942, with my mother who temporarily ran the hostel for a year. This immediately followed 2a.

3. Thorn Cottage, second stay, from summer 1944 until approximately October 1944, without my mother. The letters

indicate that my family had a holiday at Coombe Martin, Devon from 19th August to 2nd September. I then returned to Alton, but a letter from me (dated 24th September 1944) was written from the YWCA (presumably my mother was with me - but why were we there?)

4. Thorn Cottage, third stay, from January until March/April 1945, without my mother. In March 1945 the family moved to 'Bradbrook', Queen's Roads, Alton.

I shall devote one chapter to Thorn Cottage, but I suspect the large majority of my memories belong to the second and third of these stays. The subsequent chapter is devoted to the YWCA and the last to memories of London.

Thorn Cottage

At Thorn Cottage lived Aunty Chris and Aunty Bess. The former was married and her husband (Uncle Albert) worked in London but visited most weekends. Their daughter, a teacher (Aunty Dorothy), also lived there as well as Aunty Chris's grandson, Robin, whom the two aunts were bringing up and who was two years younger than me. There was also Evelyn, the teenage helper (or maid), who worked part-time and lived nearby. I loved to help her in the kitchen and sometimes she took me and Robin out.

I remember first arriving at the house, although I was only 4½ years old. My mother and I had arrived by train after a very slow journey from London, due to enemy planes overhead during an air raid. We took a taxi from the station and were only in it for what seemed a few seconds when we pulled up outside a large white house and Aunty Chris, whom I had not met before, came out to greet us and commented on how ill and pale I looked.

Thorn Cottage was a large house with rather a jumble of rooms downstairs, but upstairs it was more spacious. There was that wonderful long corridor, which stretched right from the toilet at the back to the front window. This was our train. The toilet was the driver's cab. If I stood on the lavatory seat I could look out of the square window just like a driver of an electric train. What was even more exciting was that I could see real trains from my cab and this created the perfect atmosphere. The chair at the other end of our corridor train was the guard's seat, occupied by Robin. We travelled hundreds of miles on our train, which stopped at every station so that the guard would not become restless. Unfortunately, however, some awkward people insisted on interrupting our journeys by wanting to use the driver's cab as a toilet!

Then there was Robin's bedroom - at least I think it was, but I cannot be quite certain. The bed was our bomber plane. Robin was the pilot on top of the bed, and I was the bomb-aimer, lying under the bed. Many raids were made over Germany. At one point we would've got shot down but for the brilliant manoeuvring of the controls by the pilot. But credit to me also - I was a good bomb-aimer, nearly always smack on target. Our usual plane was a Halifax (my cousin, Bill, flew in these), but we were very adaptable because it was sometimes a Lancaster, Stirling, Whitley or Fortress.

Planes were our main interest, and I had several identification books. If we saw a strange plane it was full speed ahead to identify it before it disappeared out of sight. I clearly remember doing this when we spotted a seaplane and we decided it was a Walrus. How slowly those planes moved. I can see now a Whitley bomber flying low over the town: a long, square-shaped fuselage, so heavy looking, with twin fins and rudders and so low that the pilot could be seen - what excitement! And what magic-sounding names some planes had - Messerschmitt, Junkers 88, Stuka, Dornier, Lysander, Liberator, Fortress - and what amazing shapes, like the slender Hampden, the large-nosed Boston, the clumsy Stirling, the twin-tailed Lightning and the slender curves of the Spitfire. I loved the various camouflage colours but, most of all, the magical yellow training planes.

The garden was large; not very long but very wide. Over to one side was our garden - some bushes, a few unused flower beds and a tree. That tree was our outdoor plane. The top of the tree was the pilot's position and lower down the bomb-aimer's. This was marvellous because we were really in the air and real earth bombs could be dropped. If Robin was not with me, this plane was a fighter and I was the pilot - generally of a Spitfire. Ah, the noise of a Spitfire. I can hear its whistling engine now, and I was good at imitating it. Of course, as a fighter pilot you have to control the plane and fire the guns - requiring smaller pieces of earth.

The front garden had several trees. Mr Christmas was the gardener and he always picked up the autumn leaves with two short planks of wood. This fascinated me, so I used to imitate this myself. Together, Mr Christmas and I produced a magnificent heap of leaves. This was marvellous for playing with - not to bury ourselves or to destruct the heap, but for crashing our planes into. Robin and I had many Dinky toy planes and we would act out air battles, but the difficulty was how we could crash our planes without breaking them. The very answer: the heap of leaves. The planes would even half-disappear into the heap, just like real planes when they crash into a field. I remember that one prized yellow plane completely disappeared in the leaves and, although we both searched for it, it was never found. I wonder what happened to it?

I was never an overtly aggressive child, but I well remember expressing my aggression by drawing battle scenes. Generally they were air and sea battles with a convoy of ships being attacked by German planes and English fighters coming to the rescue. What pleasure I would feel when drawing a burning plane plunging into the sea so that only the tail could be seen and the pilot was completely submerged. Or, similarly, a small part of a sinking ship being visible with all that was life beneath sea. I would sometimes play at being a pilot in a crashing plane which plunged into the sea. I would then crawl under a large silk square, representing the sea, which we frequently played with, and this would cause me great excitement.

During Christmas 1940, my mother and I stayed at a local farm (Will Hall Farm, which we called Stacey's Farm) and we were joined by my father, my mother's sister and her two boys (Aunty Kath and my cousins Howard and Keith), my grandfather (Gramps) together with Mrs Hall (his housekeeper). I can clearly remember a large decorated Christmas tree and my present of a toy London trolleybus, which I have still got. On the farm were horses, which my cousins rode. Howard (four years older) also stopped at Thorn Cottage from October 1940 until March 1941. My memory of this is very vague, but I remember making a very large snowman with him and Robin by rolling a snowball along the main road pavement. Another snowball became the head. We added a nose, mouth and eyes and our snowman seemed to last for weeks.

In the summer of 1941 (probably the school holidays) my mother and I met up again with Aunty Kath and the boys when we stayed with them in Bath for six weeks. Near to where we lived was a large, recently constructed reservoir full of water to be used in the event of fire from enemy bombing. It was very close to the houses and was like a magnet to the children of the area - and we joined them (sadly the city was bombed in the following April). I also remember being upstairs on a bus when it pulled up sharply and a man put his hand through a window and we all had to get off. When we were in the garden of the Bath house we used to communicate over the fence with the children next door. Part of the fence collapsed on top of my right hand and I lost a fingernail (and it is still out of shape even now!) Every evening before bed we listened to the radio - I clearly recall the weekly Sunday variety programme *Happidrome*.

During my later period at Thorn Cottage, Robin and I would often go out for walks. My favourite was down Richard's Lane, so named by us because Robin's friend Richard lived there. For a short time we both used to go to Richard's mother for our schooling. Anyway, Richard's Lane went gradually downhill and under the railway bridge. We always stopped there and waited for a train to pass overhead. What excitement as we heard it getting nearer and nearer until the deafening noise of it crossing the bridge - how large, how close, how green. It was so much better when it was going towards London - near to mum and dad. Further down the lane was an old disused mill, so marvellously magical and unreal. There was the stream, where we would paddle and pull our boats between the buttercups, and stretching up from this was our own Jack and Jill's hill where in the summer months we would chase up and down and have picnics.

My first and only memory of stealing stays vividly in my mind. Robin had a picture book of various trains, which had been so well used that several pages had fallen out, including my favourite picture of a London underground train arriving at a station. On one occasion he left this picture in the living room and took the rest of the book with him. When alone, I hid this picture under the sofa. Robin came back later saying he had lost it. I even helped him look for it. He gave up in the end and at a convenient moment I smuggled the beloved picture upstairs by hiding it under my pullover. Why did I do this, I now ask? I never remember taking anything from Robin again. Was it that my interest in London trains made this picture part of my home and the possession of it established a link with home?

During my second and third stays, when my mother was not with me, she would visit me on alternate weekends. How I longed for those visits. How I enjoyed them, but how I cried when she returned home. Often I would go to the station and tearfully stand on the platform and wave farewell to my mother, continuing to wave until the train turned a distant corner. Another fortnight to wait.

It was at Alton that I started school at 4½ years old. I well remember that first day. My mother took me but I did not want to stop. How I yelled when she left me. I must have been crying for half the morning. There were two sisters, twins I think, who were very kind to me by comforting me. Also there was Pam, the eldest girl in the school. All the children, right from my age up to school-leaving age, were together in a large room. There was a coal fire and on the mantelpiece were those wonderful rubbers - a tin of them and most were of two colours, white and orange. If only I could have one of those magic rubbers and use the orange end, I used to wish. Why the fascination? I do not know for definite, but I think the teacher, Miss Fielder, whom I recall was always smoking, used them a lot and this captivated me. I also remember seeing a huge spider in the toilet, which was located outside, and I refused to do the necessary.

I had several friends, but in particular Simon and my namesake. Sometimes they used to call for me in the morning and accompany me to school. Once I was invited to a birthday party and I had to wear that terrible silk blouse - ugh! This looked like a girl's blouse, but my mother assured me it was a boy's and that I looked very smart. I was not convinced - what anxiety! I hated it but did not really want to upset my mother. On another occasion, I was taken to a party by my mother and refused to go in, and nobody could manage to persuade me otherwise. My, how I got told off when we arrived home!

During my last stay I attended Alton Junior School for a few months. Our next-door neighbour, Miss Holland, was my teacher. I liked her but the work was so easy. I had done it all in my school in London. It was here that I received the cane for the first and only time - one stroke on the hand. I cannot remember why. I think it must have been for playing about with my friend Edward, who fascinated me by carrying a small box that was always full of white pieces of chewing gum. He used to spend nearly all his pocket money on this. Needless to say, it was not long before I had a similar little box. I was transferred to a new class (was this for a short time after the Easter holiday 1945, before going home?) and I hated it. The picture in my mind of my teacher is that of a witch. I did not like being with unknown children and decidedly not with the new teacher, nor did I like the new work. When my mother arrived one weekend I was determined to see her alone and tell her that I hated the school and wanted to come home. The only place I could see her alone was when she visited the toilet - but at least I told her my feelings and I think they had some bearing on my return to London soon afterwards.

Gramps (my mother's father) came to stay in Alton for a time with Mrs Hall (his housekeeper). I think several of his hardware shops in London had been bombed and he needed a break. So during the school lunch break I used to go to Gramps' flat for a meal (I liked Mrs Hall's cooking), although quite often Gramps was absent because he went to work in London. My diary often mentions that I went to church on Sundays with Gramps and Mrs Hall. I enjoyed his company.

Even at Thorn Cottage we did not completely escape the war. I clearly recall the shutters over the windows being closed when a lone German plane fired on Alton railway station and we were hustled under the stairs. During my second stay a V-1 flying bomb was heard, but fortunately it passed over. I also remember being out with my mother and returning on a bus when there was an air raid. There was a great deal of anti-aircraft gunfire and we were so glad when we eventually reached Thorn Cottage. On another occasion, a

German fighter plane was shot down nearby. What excitement when the battered Messerschmitt 109 was put on display in front of the Alton House Hotel.

YWCA

My mother took on the job of being the secretary and cook of Alton's YWCA and I went with her. This was for approximately a year (most of 1942), about an equal period either side of my sixth birthday.

It was a large house in the main road and we occupied a spacious front bedroom, which overlooked a church and a row of old cottages. There was a woman who lived in one of these who had brilliant ginger hair and my mother used to comment on how attractive it was. Ginger hair often attracts me now and I am sure this stems back to the occasions when we were looking out of the window and would see this woman. There was also a crumbling wall with many bricks missing. What a fascination this was. I can picture it now: I used to build my toy bricks in the likeness of the wall and would also find satisfaction in drawing a wall in this state.

They were a friendly group of women, or 'girls' as my mother called them, at the YWCA. Some of them were in the Women's Land Army ('Land Girls' working on local farms). There was Hilda, who was huge, spoke loudly and wore glasses. I often used to take her an early morning cup of tea.

There was also Lorna, who was much more petite. When she ate her boiled potatoes she only chewed about three times and then swallowed. I tried this no end of times, but my potato was still too lumpy to swallow. Then there was Miss Cann, whom I think was older than most of the others. Each morning I would take her a glass of hot water, and before my mother and I left the YWCA she gave me a book about a squirrel (which I still have) in appreciation of this. I cannot remember much about Miss Alexander except that she was thin with dark hair. Edna was the helper or maid. She was full of life and acted more like a boy with her well-built, strong, athletic body. I suppose her face was not very feminine - but I liked her. My favourite, however, was June, a land girl. I suppose she was still a teenager. She used to wear a green jumper and had fairly long dark hair but, strange to say, I don't have a clear picture of her face. I think she had rather thin lips, brown eyes and a pleasant countenance and, although probably not a raving beauty, she was easily my favourite. I would call her 'Junny' and she would chase me. This was what I wanted. Well, no it wasn't - what I really wanted was for her to catch me. Then she would pull me onto the floor and tickle me. This was best during the summer months when I would run out into the garden and she would roll me over on the grass. It was imperative that nobody else was watching or this would spoil everything. She would then generally carry me in. How warm and comforting was her green jumper. Sometimes she would have a rough and tumble with Edna, who was too rough for me, and this made jealousy loom up inside me. I wanted to play with June. I suppose she was my first girlfriend in the sense that she emotionally excited me. Yet I cannot recall being upset when we left (or did June leave first?) or any fretting for her.

I enjoyed my time at the YWCA, and I think after leaving there my mother and I probably returned to London. Later evacuation was more unsettling for me - no mother with me, no secure companionship as experienced at the hostel, homesickness, and several unsuccessful attempts at living back in London (because I found the air raids too stressful). I did, however, enjoy the friendship of Robin and we played well together. I loved the company of Evelyn, and the aunts did their very best for me, but it was not the same as home.

It was a paradoxical situation. I wanted to be home in London, but when there were bad air raids I wanted to escape to Alton, and yet, once there, I was homesick and wanted to return to London - a situation destined to cause stress and anxiety. Some effects of this are shown in the previous chapter on Thorn Cottage and in my letters to my father (see page four and also the final chapter).

Despite this, as an only child I most definitely gained a great deal from the varied social experiences of evacuation, and I am also sure that my present love of the countryside stems from this period of my life.

LETTERS

There were 36 letters relating to my evacuation amongst my late father's private papers. Of these, 26 were written by me to home, 8 to me from my father and 2 from my mother. My letters gave me a clearer understanding and insight into my own feelings. I was obviously homesick, as I kept referring to relatives, friends, pets and toys and always asked about recent bombs, rockets, etc. There were frequent requests for my toys, books and comics to be sent to me.

As an adult who has worked with children, I now appreciate the 'classic' letters my father wrote - just what a child away from home wants. I note his constant mention of my friends, relations, toys (e.g., my barrage balloon), pets and other interests (e.g., music, drum kit), and he even enclosed a sample of the family cat's fur. The mention of the new Morrison shelter would have lessened my concern about air raids. They contain so much loving praise and encouragement.

MEANWHILE - BACK IN LONDON

In between periods of evacuation, I was back home in London. Evidence from one of my father's letters indicates that I came home for a day on 17th June 1941 (I am not sure why, but it's possible it was linked to my birthday on the 19th).

Other than this, there were four periods of being at home:

1. Early 1940 until autumn 1940. I have no significant memories of this period.
2. All of 1943 up until summer 1944.
3. October 1944 up until January 1945.
4. March/April 1945 until the end of the war (VE Day - 8th May 1945).

Memories are vague prior to early 1944, by which time I was 7½ years old. I can remember attending the local infants school (I would have left it in July 1943) and the kindly headmistress, Miss McCormick. Similarly, I remember attending the junior school and the tall, elegant figure of Mr Wilson, the headmaster. In the event of an air-raid warning, lessons would be held in the purpose-built shelters in the playground. The deafening but friendly noise of the anti-aircraft guns in Finsbury Park would start. All this upheaval and escape from work was a novelty at first, but that soon wore off - the shelters were damp, cold, smelled of cement, and were too small and uncomfortable.

My father was an ARP warden (Air Raid Precautions) and the 'post' was directly opposite our house - a small, square, concrete structure. He had regular times on duty, often all night, and the other wardens always seemed to be friendly towards me and towards each other - there was a real sense of camaraderie. They were responsible for air raid casualties - rescuing, first aid, calling the necessary emergency services, etc, as well as routine patrols to check no house lights coud be seen (all houses had to have blackout blinds so enemy aircraft had no visable targets).

This reminds me of the time that Uncle Albert, Robin's Grandfather from Alton, stayed with us in London for several weeks during spring 1944. I remember him as an active elderly man who worked at the Admiralty in London. Every morning, punctually at 7 am, he had a cold bath. One morning he misread the time thinking it was nearly 7.10 am but it was only 1.35 am. The bath was prepared and he pulled up the blackout blinds in the bathroom and his bedroom not realising it was still dark outside. In no time wardens were knocking on the front door shouting, “Put those lights out!” My father was not on duty that night but how embarrassed he was - and so was Uncle Albert! Fortunately, however, there was no air raid at the time and a sense of humour prevailed.

Clearer memories of the time, and their associated emotions, stem from early 1944. I remember my father carrying me out of the front door to show me the results of the firebombing of an area only a mile away (I now know it was Sunday 19th February 1944 at about 1.30 a.m.) The sky was alight. In one way it was beautiful, like a summer sunset or sunrise, but in another it was a terrible scene of destruction as houses and shops burned. My father knew it included Wilson’s, a large department store (he must have been on night duty). I can remember feeling amazement tinged with fear, and I was glad to return to the safety of my house. The picture of the scene clearly remains with me.

Barrage balloons fascinated me. I am not sure if I knew at the time what they were for (i.e., to serve as obstacles to low-flying enemy aircraft), but they were wonderful silver shapes peacefully and passively floating in the sky. Most of the ones around us were based in parks and I knew which balloons came from which parks. They were raised to one of three heights - low, medium and high. There were ropes hanging from each side of the balloon and one at the back. These could be hanging loosely or (except for the back one) they could be joined together beneath the balloon in a V shape. In some cases a few were tied together and the rest hung loosely. What a fascination this was for me.

I had my own toy barrage balloon located outside at the foot of our pear tree. With the aid of a pulley it was hauled up into the tree to one of three heights just like the real balloons. Once at the top of the tree, it was as if it were up in the clouds. When I was in London the balloon was positioned every day. I recall getting severely reprimanded when the air-raid siren sounded and, instead of sheltering in the cellar, I rushed out into the garden to hoist my barrage balloon as high as possible. I bet the real barrage balloon crews didn't get told off!

I have clear memories of watching allied bombers flying southwards on bombing missions. We used to go into the garden in an attempt to identify the planes (mainly four-engine American Fortresses and Liberators on daylight raids) and count them. There were often hundreds of them, creating a tremendous droning noise and I am sure taking at least twenty minutes to pass over. We would also try to estimate the number of airmen up there, bearing in mind that each aircraft contained an average of nine personnel. Hours later we would be awaiting their return and rushed out into the garden at the first sound of an aircraft. We would count them again and tot up the number missing. If a large number were missing we were generally silent. But we would still wait and often another few would follow - probably damaged and unable to keep up with the rest. Sometimes there was a long gap and then we would see a lone bomber struggling back, flying low, perhaps with an engine not working, and we would cheer, hoping it would reach home safely.

One evening (it was early April 1944) I had just settled into bed when my father entered the room looking upset - in fact I had never seen him looking so distressed. He sat down beside the bed and told me that Bill, my cousin in RAF Bomber Command, had been reported missing on a bombing raid over Germany. I felt no emotion and felt guilty for this, especially as my father was so upset. However, the following day the realisation of what my father had said dawned on me. (Subsequently we heard that Bill was a Prisoner of War - and he survived the war.)

I can hear my father saying in mid-June 1944, "There's talk of a German pilotless plane", and can remember thinking -

that's impossible. This marked the beginning of my biggest fear of the war - the V-1, doodlebug or buzz bomb. The sound of one of these still makes my stomach turn over - that dreaded, deep throbbing sound that got closer and closer and louder and louder. You hoped it would pass over and the sound would disappear before the engine cut and it plunged to earth with an almighty explosion. Sometimes the engine cut long before it reached us, but the explosion was still loud, even more so in the middle of the night. At night I was always awakened by the sound of a V-1 - it seemed so much louder and more eerie than during the day. I can recollect seeing one in the daytime flying northwards - not very high and belching flames from its rear. However, it was travelling quickly away from us and I felt no fear.

One night I was sleeping downstairs with most of my body tucked under my father's desk (that is where I slept during an air raid) when I was awakened by this fearful, horrific, deep throbbing sound of a V-1. It got closer, closer, closer, until it was right overhead and the whole house vibrated. Then the engine cut. I held my breath, curling into a tight embryonic position with my heart pounding as if to burst. Then there was an enormous explosion and the sound of breaking glass - the whole house shook but remarkably none of our windows broke. The next morning we heard it had landed in nearby Finsbury Park with apparently no casualties but leaving an enormous crater. That V-1 sound and those ten or so seconds after the engine cut are still with me and will never fade. This event resulted in my returning to Alton (second stay, by myself) and soon after my father acquired a Morrison shelter - a steel table with an opening on one side under which two or three could sleep or shelter.

Two V-1s fell in Finsbury Park (25th June and 4th July) but it was probably the first as the second fell at 5.30 p.m. and there were reports of 38 casualties at the anti-aircraft gun site. I can also recall one evening when a V-1 passed over and we relaxed when the sound faded away into the distance. A minute or so later there was a loud 'swishing' noise followed by an enormous explosion. The monster's engine had cut out about six to eight miles away, but it had then turned and silently glided back, exploding about half a mile away. It was a Sunday evening (10th December 1944) and my father was playing the organ at our local Congregational Church about a third of a mile away when this landed (quite near the church). Part of the church ceiling came down. My father immediately rushed out of the church fearful for our safety back at home. Nearby houses had many broken windows, but as he hurried back he was relieved to find that the closer he got to home the less damage he could see. The V-1 had fallen on the other side of the church.

I was awakened very late that evening by friends of ours knocking on the front door. That V-1 had destroyed their house and several others in Fairfax Road and they wanted us to take them in. There was no question about it - we did, and anyone else would have done so. They (mother, father and two teenage girls) were grey all over from the dust that had been blasted over them. They were given tea and offered hot baths. I don't remember any of them being hurt, but I do remember the father staying with us for several weeks and enjoying his company. (The rest of the family probably moved out of London for a time but the father, a railway worker, had to remain because of his work.)

Hot on the heels of the V-1 flying bombs came the V-2 rockets, which caused an even louder explosion. I was never in fear of these because there wasn't the same slow build-up up of fear as with the monster doodlebug - the V-2s just came. I remember one morning (10th November 1944) I was getting ready for school at about 8.15 a.m. and was in my parents' upstairs front bedroom where my father was still in bed (perhaps he had been on ARP night duty). Suddenly there was an enormous explosion and some of the front room windows crashed in as a result of the blast. It was a V-2 rocket, which had landed about half a mile away, and it caused a great number of casualties (10 killed and 78 injured). I think school was cancelled that day.

In my 1945 diary I wrote that I was going on Wednesday 3rd January to Alton and returning on Monday 8th in order to return to school for the beginning of a new term on the Tuesday. I did not return because of the V-1s and V-2s, but it is only recently that I discovered that on the day I was due to return a V-2 fell about a quarter of a mile from my home in London, destroying 14 houses and seriously damaging 70 others, with the casualty figures of 14 killed and 99 injured. This must have been the reason for my staying in Alton (my third stay).

I was home again before VE (Victory in Europe) day on 8th May 1945. I remember my parents telling me that the war had ended and there would be no more air raids or sirens. There was so much relief - I couldn't believe it. Up until that point in my life I had known nothing but the fear of war and an unsettled existence, although I hasten to add that I had not had an unhappy childhood. VE day was celebrated with a street party for all the children (I have still got the photographs) and

I think a dance in the evening for the adults in the local school hall.

When VJ (Victory in Japan) day came on 15th August 1945 I was on holiday with my parents in Salcombe, Devon. There were many celebrations - dancing, parties and sports - and holidaymakers were made most welcome. I remember entering a running race (100 yards) for 8/9-year-olds (I was just 9 years old at that time). There must have been about 40 or so children in the race and I appeared to be about the shortest, but to everyone's surprise I won and I clearly recall a policeman picking me out as the winner and receiving my prize (saving stamps to the value of 7s 6d - I still have the card). The VJ celebrations were more memorable and exciting for me, but were definitely not accompanied by that emotional relief and peace of mind on VE day.

EVACUEES EXHIBITION IMPERIAL WAR MUSEUM

During 1995 I answered a newspaper letter from the Imperial War Museum, London, requesting memorabilia/ artefacts associated with the evacuation of children during the Second World War. This was for a forthcoming exhibition at the museum.

My letter received a prompt telephone reply and an enthusiastic voice was keen to borrow wartime toys and books. I was surprised to hear of a shortage of books of the period, as apparently most people had discarded them. There was also an interest in the 36 wartime letters found among my late father's papers, which I shall mention later, but the museum had sufficient available for the exhibition.

I lent the museum 32 items, comprising 9 toys (6 buses, 2 aircraft and a barrage balloon), 22 books and the sheet music of the song 'Goodnight Children Everywhere'. In the exhibition, 23 of these were displayed (6 toys, 16 books and the sheet music).

The museum was thrilled to receive the sheet music as a specific search had been made for this. The song was written in late 1939 specifically for evacuated children. It is thought that the title is based on the farewell words of 'Uncle Mac' (Derek McCulloch) at the end of every *Children's Hour*, a very popular daily radio programme. The song was recorded by Gracie Fields and there were two versions by Vera Lynn (late 1939 and 1940).

The Evacuees exhibition opened on 14th March 1996, but I and my wife Annette received an invitation to a private viewing and official opening on the evening of 13th March.

All former evacuees were asked to wear a label, which was compulsory when children were evacuated through government schemes, stating where they had been evacuated (see illustration of leaflet and label). We were offered wine or orange juice and nibbles and had an opportunity to talk to museum staff.

Next we were gathered for the formal opening, which was very appropriately performed by Dame Vera Lynn. This was a thrill for me as I have a great interest in the popular music of the time. She spoke of the immense difficulties faced by many children during the war and was pleased that this was now being recognised.

We were then given the opportunity to look around the exhibition. It was very thorough, with many theme displays and a number of rooms decked out in the decor of the period. Information was clearly displayed and acknowledgements were given to those who had loaned items. In one room the acknowledgement to me was, 'Items loaned by Graham Inward, who was evacuated on four different occasions'. A lady behind me read this and said with great emotion, "Oh that poor little boy was evacuated four times." My wife could not resist the opportunity of saying to her, "That little boy is standing in front of you." She looked at me, but her expression did not match the emotion of her remark.

I clearly remember the section on overseas evacuation, especially a letter from a young girl who was sent to Canada. She was so homesick that in this emotional letter to her parents she threatened to run away from where she was living and swim home. I wonder what happened to her?

Most left the exhibition having had vivid memories recalled - some sad, some happy. All were agreed about the high standard of the exhibition and what a learning experience this would be for those with no memories of the war, especially for visiting school pupils.

We were standing in the large and lofty main entrance of the Imperial War Museum when we saw Dame Vera Lynn standing alone beside an army tank. "I'm going to ask her for her autograph," I said to Annette, and I promptly went across and asked her if she would sign my invitation card. She willingly did so. I told her that I had loaned the sheet music of 'Goodnight Children Everywhere', which was displayed next to her loaned master record of the song sung by her (see photograph with my Grandson Jordan). This was a conversation starter. I told her that I had a copy of her record, which was accompanied by an organ, but that I also had another record of her singing the song with the famous dance band led by Ambrose. She was surprised at this, as even she herself had not got a copy. It was recorded after the organ recording of December 1939. By now Dame Vera had been noticed by many people and a queue was forming for her autograph, and I had had more than my fair share of her. What a charming, friendly and ordinary person she is. I will always remember that evening of nostalgia with great joy, highlighted, of course, by that conversation with Dame Vera Lynn.

The Evacuees exhibition was a great success, so much so that it was extended from its original closing date of 27th October 1996 to 5th January 1997, and then further extended to 31st March 1997. My loaned items were returned in May.

Meanwhile the museum wrote to me asking for a copy of the

account of my wartime years and whether I would donate the 36 wartime letters to the museum. The former was no problem, but I simply could not agree to the latter as this would mean giving up ownership of these letters, which were too precious to me to part with and were the strongest link I had with my father (see Postscript). The museum accepted this and requested photocopies instead. This presented no difficulties, so in early July 1997 I again visited the museum with my written account, and the letters were duly photocopied and stored in their archives.

In March 2001, I received a letter from the museum archivist informing me that a Mr Stephen Darlow was writing a book on how RAF Bomber Command destroyed V-1 flying-bomb sites because of the suffering they were inflicting on the population of Southern England. At the start of some chapters he wanted to include examples of how civilians were being affected and had asked for my permission to quote from my childhood account of when I was frightened during the night by a flying bomb that landed nearby. I wrote to Stephen Darlow giving him my authorisation to do so. The book, *Sledgehammers for Tintacks* was published in 2002.

APPENDIX 1
BREAKDOWN OF TIME

Evacuation:

* Stage 1 - Wisbech/Cambridge - 4 months

(early September 1939 until early 1940)

* Stage 2a - Alton, Thorn Cottage (and Bath) - 15 months

(autumn 1940 until December 1941)

* Stage 2b - Alton YWCA - 11 months

(early 1942 until December 1942)

* Stage 3 - Alton, Thorn Cottage (2nd stay) - 4 months

(summer 1944 until October 1944)

* Stage 4 - Alton, Thorn Cottage (3rd stay) - 3 months

(January 1945 until March/April 1945)

London:

* Stage 1 - 9 months

(early 1940 until autumn 1940)

* Stage 2 - 18 months

(all of 1943 until summer 1944)

* Stage 3 - 3 months

(October 1944 until January 1945)

* Stage 4 - 1 month (VE day); 4 months (VJ day) (March/April 1945 until the end of the war)

EVACUATION: 3 years 1 month

LONDON: 2 years 7 months to VE day; 2 years 10 months to VJ day

APPENDIX 2
WARTIME SCHOOLS

* April 1941 to December 1942: Miss Fielder (Alton)

* January 1943 to July 1943: South Harringay Infants School (London)

* September 1943 to summer 1944: South Harringay Junior School (London)

* Summer 1944 to July 1944: Mrs Holford (Alton)

(? September 1944)

* October 1944 to December 1944: South Harringay Junior School (London)

* January 1945 to March/April 1945: Alton Junior School

* March/April 1945 onwards: South Harringay Junior School (London)

POSTSCRIPT

In the late 1960s, two years after my father's death, I was on a full-time one-year course at the University of London Institute of Education studying the teaching of children with special educational needs. Part of this involved the exploration of my early childhood, so naturally this led me back to life during the war and my experience of evacuation.

This task was greatly helped by the 36 letters found among my father's private papers. These gave invaluable information and were so objective. But the 8 letters from my father to me, unseen for so many years, have caused me much reflection. I have read and reread these. This is not the same father I remember from my childhood. The letters communicate a great closeness and affection, which seldom emerged in post-war life. Why? Decidedly my mother was the dominant parent when dealing with any issues concerning me (a long-awaited only child). The two did little together and I recall her many criticisms of my father (he never criticised her).

I only remember a few 'father and son' events, such as a day trip to the Scilly Isles in 1951 when on holiday in Cornwall. We both flew in a De Havilland Dragon Rapide biplane for a wonderful day still clearly remembered. I also recall one or two visits with him to see a band or singer at the local Empire and playing buses with him. These events, however, were few and clearly he took the role of the passive parent. My mother had many interests, especially the Girl Guide movement in which she became a District Commissioner. This took up a considerable amount of her time and, unwittingly, I found myself involved in some of the social events.

Was my father carefully manipulated away from me and I, in turn, from him? Was my mother unable to share me with my father? It is significant that the evacuation letters to me from my father were always from 'mummy and daddy', whereas my mother's were only from 'mummy'. The more I reflect, the more I think this was the situation. His evacuation letters to me were 'father and son' events when he was free to write such masterpieces of closeness, encouragement and praise. His style of writing was as though he were talking to me face-to-face, and the news of my friends, pets, toys, etc., was just what a child away from home would want to hear. The enclosure of a sample of fur from the family cat and his involvement with my favourite music and my drum kit showed such insight. The letters are so positive, but, above all, he makes it clear that he missed me. It is sad to think I needed to wait until after his death before these letters enabled me to receive his true feelings.

The one-year course was of great professional benefit, but it was with very mixed emotions that I was also given this unique opportunity to meet my real father.

BIBLIOGRAPHY

Darlow, S., *Sledgehammers for Tintacks: Bomber Command Combats the V-1 Menace, 1943-1944* (Grub Street, 2002).

Wicks, Ben, *No Time to Wave Goodbye* (Bloomsbury, 1988).

Wicks, Ben, *The Day They Took the Children* (Bloomsbury, 1989).

Parsons, Martin, *I'll Take That One* (Beckett Karlson, 1998).

Parsons, M. and Starns, P., *The Evacuation* (DMS, 1999).

Holman, B., *The Evacuation: A Very British Revolution* (Lion, 1995).

Alien, E., *Wartime Children 1939-45* (Black, 1975).

Hollingsworth, H., *They Tied a Label on My Coat* (Virago, 1992).

Brown, M., *A Child's War* (Sutton Publishing, 2000).

Brown, M., *Evacuees* (Sutton Publishing, 2000).

Minns, R., *Bombers and Mash* (Past Times, 1999).

Gardiner, J., *The People's War* (Select Editions, 1991).

Reynoldson, F., *The Home Front - Evacuation* (Wayland, 1990).

Reynoldson, F., *The Home Front - The Blitz* (Wayland, 1990).

Reynoldson, F., *The Home Front - Rationing* (Wayland, 1990).

Reynoldson, F., *The Home Front - Women's War* (Wayland, 1991).

Opie, R., *The Wartime Scrapbook* (New Cavendish Books, 1995).

Unknown, *The Spirit of Wartime* (Orbis Publishing, 1995).

Lynn, Dame Vera, *We'll Meet Again* (Sidgwick & Jackson, 1989).

Kennett, Naden and Stamp, *The Day War Broke Out* (Marshall Cavendish, 1989).

Public Records Office, *Images of War: British Posters 1939-45* (HMSO, 1989).

Kelsall, F., *How We Used to Live* (Macdonald, 1981).

Lang, C., *Keep Smiling Through: Women in the Second World War* (Cambridge, 1989).

Turner, B. and Kennell, T., *When Daddy Came Home* (Pimlico, 1996).

Green, B., *Britain at War* (W. H. Smith, 1989).

Rodger, G., *The Blitz: Photographs* (Bloomsbury, 1994).

Mack, J. and Humphries, S., *London at War* (Sidgwick & Jackson, 1985).

O'Neill, G., *Our Street: East End Life in the Second World War* (Penguin, 2004).

Graves, C., *London Transport at War (1939-45)* (Almark, 1974).

Goodman, S., *Children of War* (John Murray, 2005).

Hornsey Historical Society, Home Fires: A North London Suburb at War (1992).

ORIGINAL WARTIME BOOKS etc.

Adult

Aircraft Recognition; R.Saville-Sneath (Penguin Special 1941)

Aircraft Identification, Part 1 British Monoplanes; The Aeroplane (Temple Press 1942)

Aircraft Identification, Part 2 German Monoplanes; The Aeroplane (Temple Press 1942)

The Cambridge Evacuation Survey; Ed. S. Isaacs (Methuen. 1941)

Cookery

Wartime Recipes (BBC)

Two hundred Wartime Recipes; A. Heath (Eyre & Spottiswoode 1941)

New Wartime Recipes (Good Housekeeping)

Thrifty Wartime Recipes (Good Housekeeping)

The Kitchen Front (BBC)

Gert & Daisy's Wartime Cookery Book (Withy Grove Press)

Miscellaneous

Radio Times, July 23-31 1943

Civil Defence Public Information Leaflet No.3 - Evacuation, Why and How? (1939)

National Registration Identity Cards (myself, wife and mother)

National Health & Pensions Insurance Contribution Card (1942)

Regular Unemployment Book (unemployment insurance stamps - 1942)

Sheet Music, “Goodnight Children Everywhere” (1939)

- written for evacuated children

Certificate given to all school children (June 1946) as part of the first, anniversary celebrations of the end of the war.

“Housewife” (a monthly magazine) - many copies covering the war years.

Children’s Books

Blossom the Brave Balloon; E. Herbert & P. Zec (Muller)

The ABC of London Transport Services; B. Tatford (lan Allan 1944)

The Battle of Britain; D. Garnett & J. Gardner (Puffin Picture)

The Wonder Book of Aircraft (Ward Lock)

The Wonder Book of Why and What (Ward Lock)

Knights of the Air; R. Davies (Valentine)

Aircraft of Today (Thames Publishing)

Seaplanes (Juvenile Productions)

Defenders of the Empire (Juvenile Productions)

Air Power of the Empire (Juvenile Productions)

Air War at Sea; D. Ayre (Raphael Tuck)

With the Merchant Navy; C. Jarman (Raphael Tuck)

The Might of the Empire (Birn Brothers)

Our Wonderful Empire (Birn Brothers)

Cavalcade of Ships; H.J. Shepstone (Collins)

The Story of British Railway Engines; P.A. Purton (R.A. Publishing)

The Children's How & Why Aeroplane Book; M. Adams (Faber & Faber)

Nursery Rhyme Pictures (Birn Brothers)

Panda in Farmland (Juvenile Productions)

The Bruin All Colour Picture Book (Juvenile Productions)

Kiki the Squirrel; J. Thornicroft (Harrap 1938)

Picture Book of Kittens; J. Pope (Ward Lock)

Stories of St. Paul (Blackie)

The Water Babies; retold by A. Pitt-Kethley (Routledge)

Fairy Tales from Andersen & Grimm; retold by A. Pitt-Kethley (Routledge)

The Adventures of Timothy & Peter; W. Barnes (Fairston)

THE AUTHOR
Graham Inward

Graham Inward was born in June 1936 and was living in North London at the time of the outbreak of the Second World War. His childhood through the war years was thus spent both in blitzed London and also as an evacuee on four separate occasions. Following National Service in the Royal Army Educational Corps, he spent 38 years in the teaching profession, largely working with children with special educational needs. In 1961 he married his wife Annette and they have four children and four grandchildren.

CIVIL DEFENCE

EVACUATION
WHY AND HOW?

PUBLIC INFORMATION
LEAFLET NO. 3

Read this and
keep it carefully.
You may need it.

Issued from the Lord Privy Seal's Office July, 1939

The Government prepares
for war (July 1939)

Summer 1940 in my London garden playing
my favourite role as a bus conductor -
with my mother's cat Paddy

My very own pet whom I missed so much when evacuated

Robin and I outside Thorn Cottage (1941)

A visit from Robin's friend Richard and his sister Margaret (1941)

Mother, myself, Aunty Chris, Robin and Aunty Bess in Thorn Cottage garden (1941)

Christmas 1940 at Will Hall Farm (cousins Keith and Howard, the farmer, father, Aunty Kath, Gramps, Mrs Hall, mother --- Keith was later known as John Benson the 'voice' of 'Sale of the Century' and often heard on other media programmes)

When living at the YWCA in 1942 I still made regular contact with Robin

Summer 1944
(second stay at Thorn Cottage)

The wonderful Evelyn

Robin's drawing of Thorn Cottage (the tower on the right is an air raid siren)

The stolen picture!

My identity card issued in May 1940

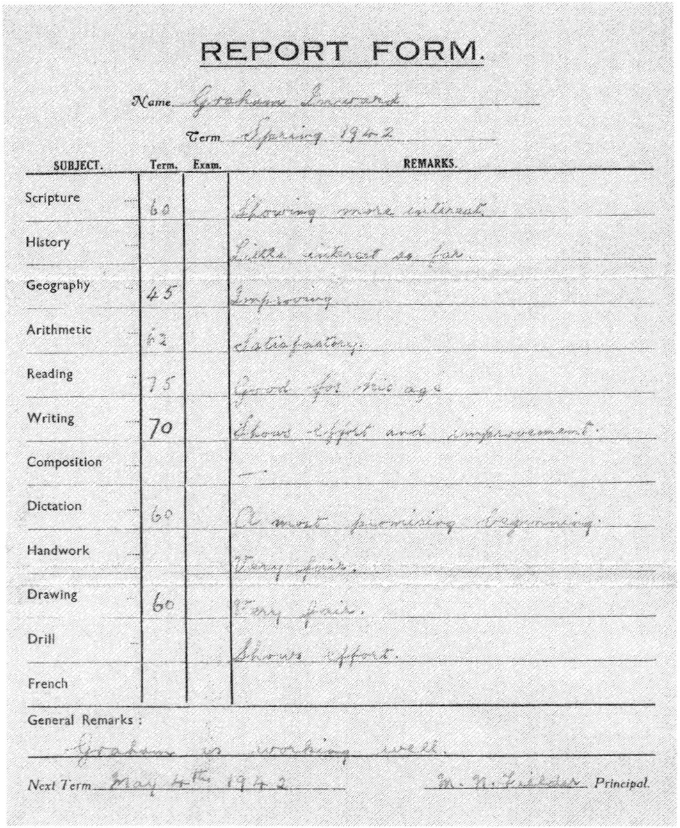

REPORT FORM.

Name: Graham Inward

Term: Spring 1942

SUBJECT.	Term.	Exam.	REMARKS.
Scripture	60		Showing more interest
History			Little interest so far.
Geography	45		Improving
Arithmetic	62		Satisfactory.
Reading	75		Good for his age
Writing	70		Shows effort and improvement.
Composition			—
Dictation	60		A most promising beginning.
Handwork			Very fair.
Drawing	60		Very fair.
Drill			Shows effort.
French			

General Remarks: Graham is working well.

Next Term: May 4th 1942 — M. N. Fielder, Principal.

School report from my first Alton school (Miss Fielder)

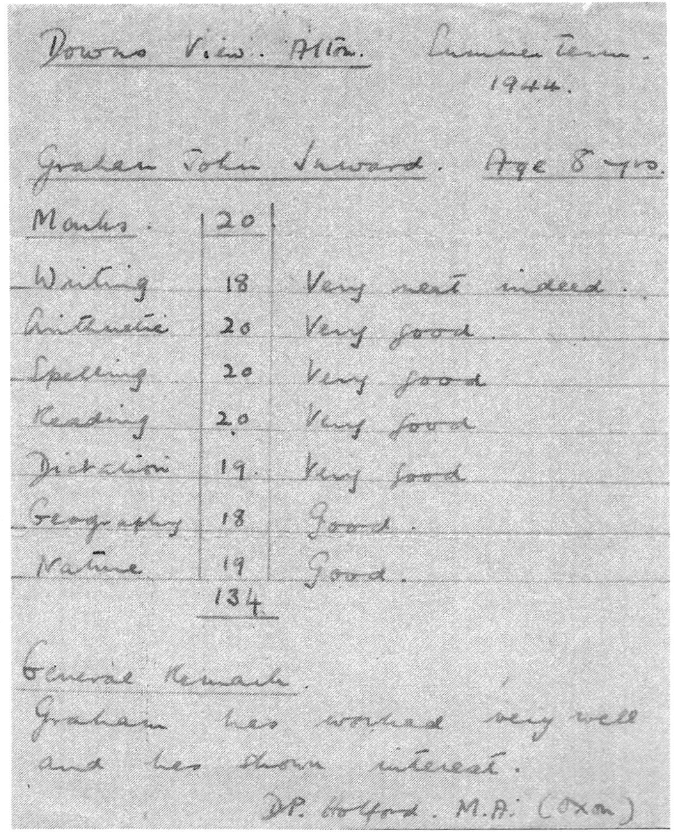

Downs View. Alton. Summer Term. 1944.

Graham John Inward. Age 8 yrs.

Marks.	20	
Writing	18	Very neat indeed.
Arithmetic	20	Very good.
Spelling	20	Very good
Reading	20	Very good
Dictation	19.	Very good
Geography	18	Good.
Nature	19	Good.
	134	

General Remark.

Graham has worked very well and has shown interest.

D.P. Holford. M.A. (Oxon)

For a few weeks in June/July 1944 I was schooled by Mrs Holford, Richard's mother

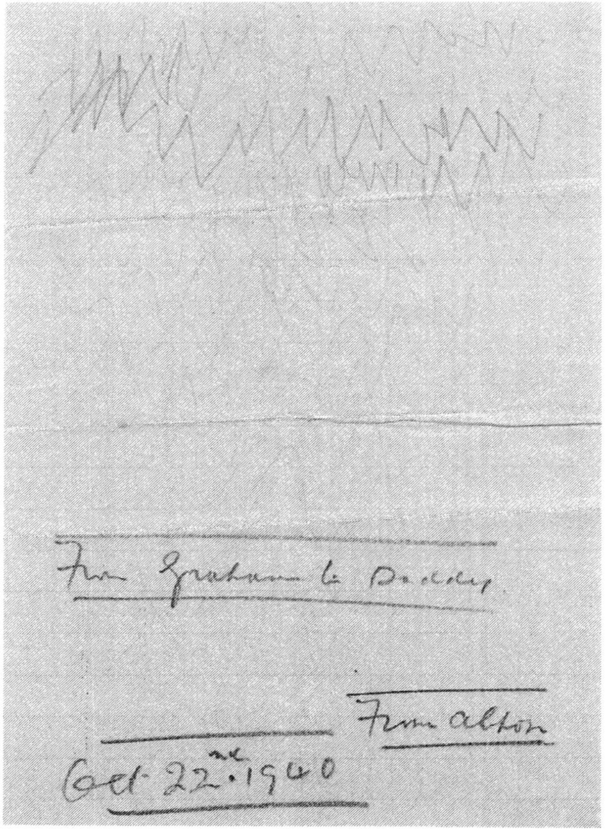

From Graham to Daddy.

From Alton

Oct 22nd 1940

My very first letter home from Thorn Cottage

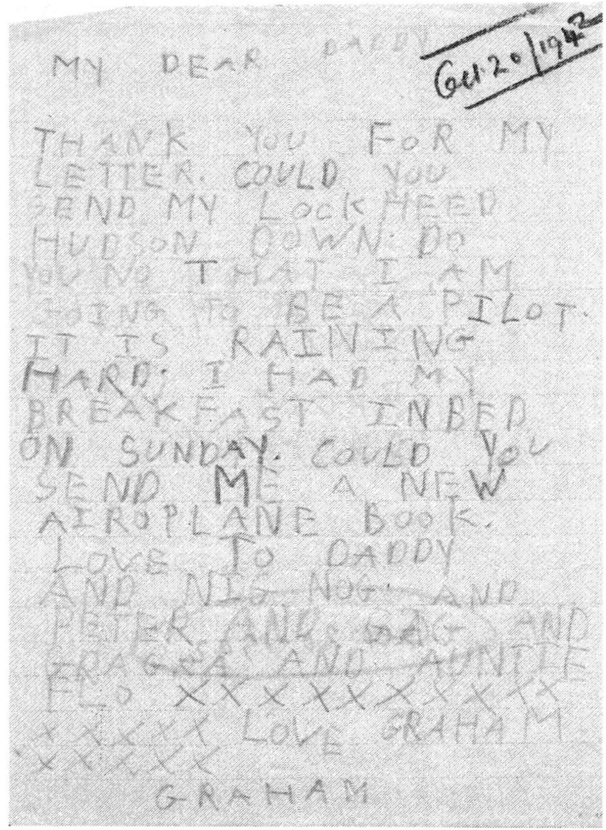

Oct 20 1942

MY DEAR DADDY

THANK YOU FOR MY LETTER. COULD YOU SEND MY LOCKHEED HUDSON DOWN. DO YOU NO THAT I AM GOING TO BE A PILOT. IT IS RAINING HARD. I HAD MY BREAKFAST IN BED ON SUNDAY. COULD YOU SEND ME A NEW AIROPLANE BOOK. LOVE TO DADDY AND NIG NOG AND PETER AND GRAGRA AND AUNTIE FLO XXXXXXXXXXXXXXXX LOVE GRAHAM XXXXXX

GRAHAM

Letter written from YWCA

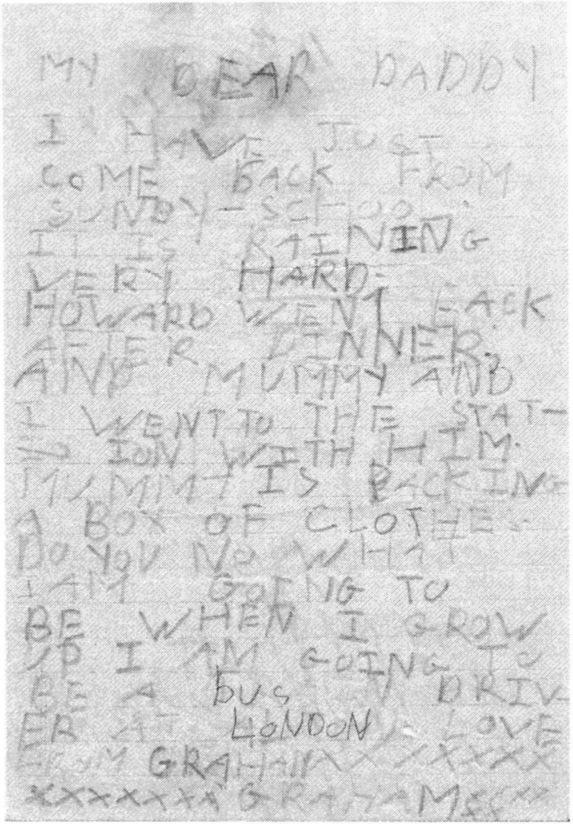

MY DEAR DADDY
I HAVE JUST
COME BACK FROM
SUNDAY-SCHOOL
IT IS RAINING
VERY HARD
HOWARD WENT BACK
AFTER DINNER
AND MUMMY AND
I WENT TO THE STAT-
ION WITH HIM.
MUMMY IS PACKING
A BOX OF CLOTHES
DO YOU NO WHAT
I AM GOING TO
BE WHEN I GROW
UP I AM GOING TO
BE A bus DRIV-
ER AT LONDON LOVE
FROM GRAHAM XXXXX
XXXXXX GRAHAM

A further letter sent from the YWCA (1942)

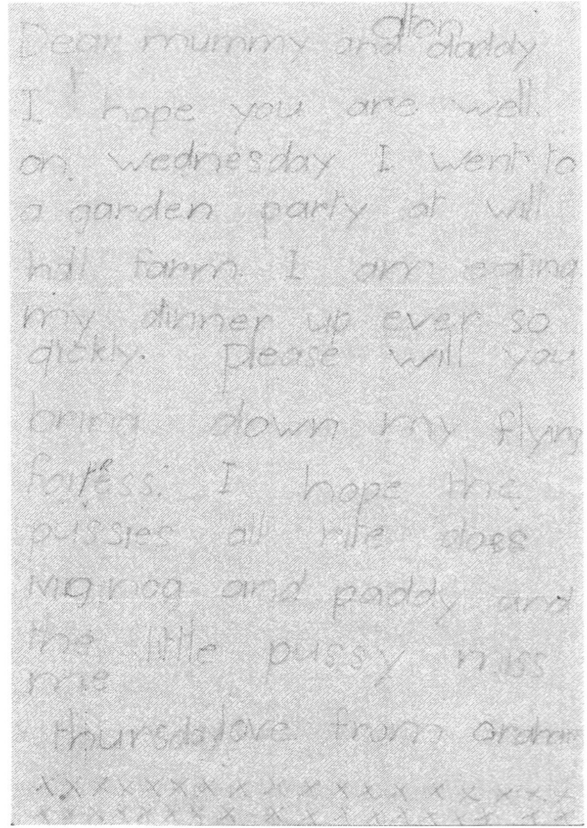

Dear mummy and daddy
I hope you are well
on wednesday I went to
a garden party at will
hill farm. I am eating
my dinner up ever so
qickly. please will you
bring down my flying
fortess. I hope the
pussies all rite does
[illegible] and paddy and
the little pussy miss
me
thursday love from graham
xxxxxxxxxxxxxxxxxx

Letter from my second stay at Thorn Cottage (late June 1944)

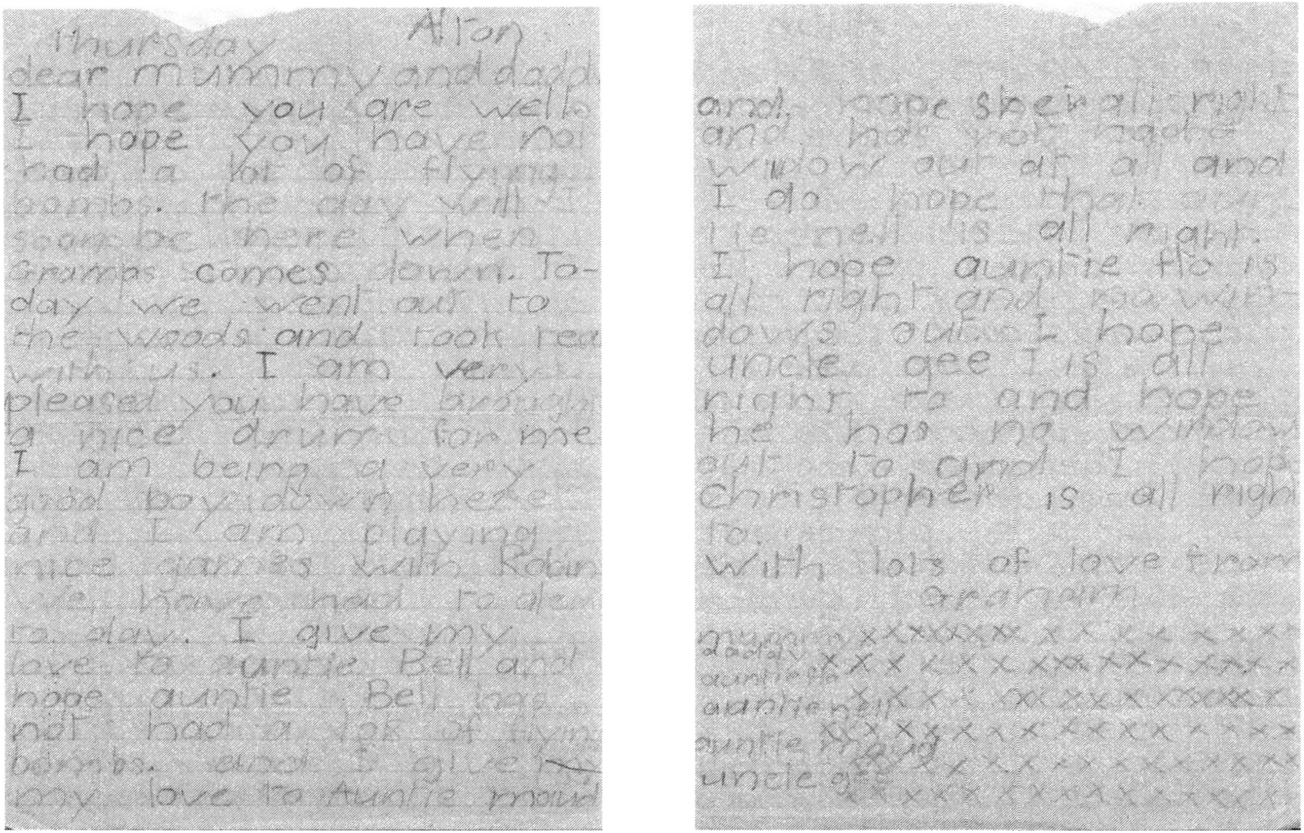

Thursday Alton
dear mummy and daddy
I hope you are well
I hope you have not
had a lot of flying
bombs. The day will I
soon be there when
Gramps comes down. To-
day we went out to
the woods and took tea
with us. I am very
pleased you have brought
a nice drum for me
I am being a very
good boy down here
and I am playing
nice games with Robin
we have had to [illegible]
to day. I give my
love to auntie Bell and
hope auntie Bell has
not had a lot of flying
bombs. and I give my
my love to Auntie maud

and hope she is all right
and has not had the
window out at all and
I do hope that [illegible]
lie nell is all right.
I hope auntie flo is
all right and no win-
dows out. I hope
uncle gee I is all
right to and hope
he has no window
out to and I hope
christopher is all right
to.
With lots of love from
graham
mummy xxxxxxxxxxxxxx
daddy xxxxxxxxxxxxxx
auntie flo xxxxxxxxxxxxxx
auntie bell xxxxxxxxxxxxxx
auntie maud xxxxxxxxxxxxxx
uncle gee xxxxxxxxxxxxxx

Letter from Thorn Cottage (late summer 1944)

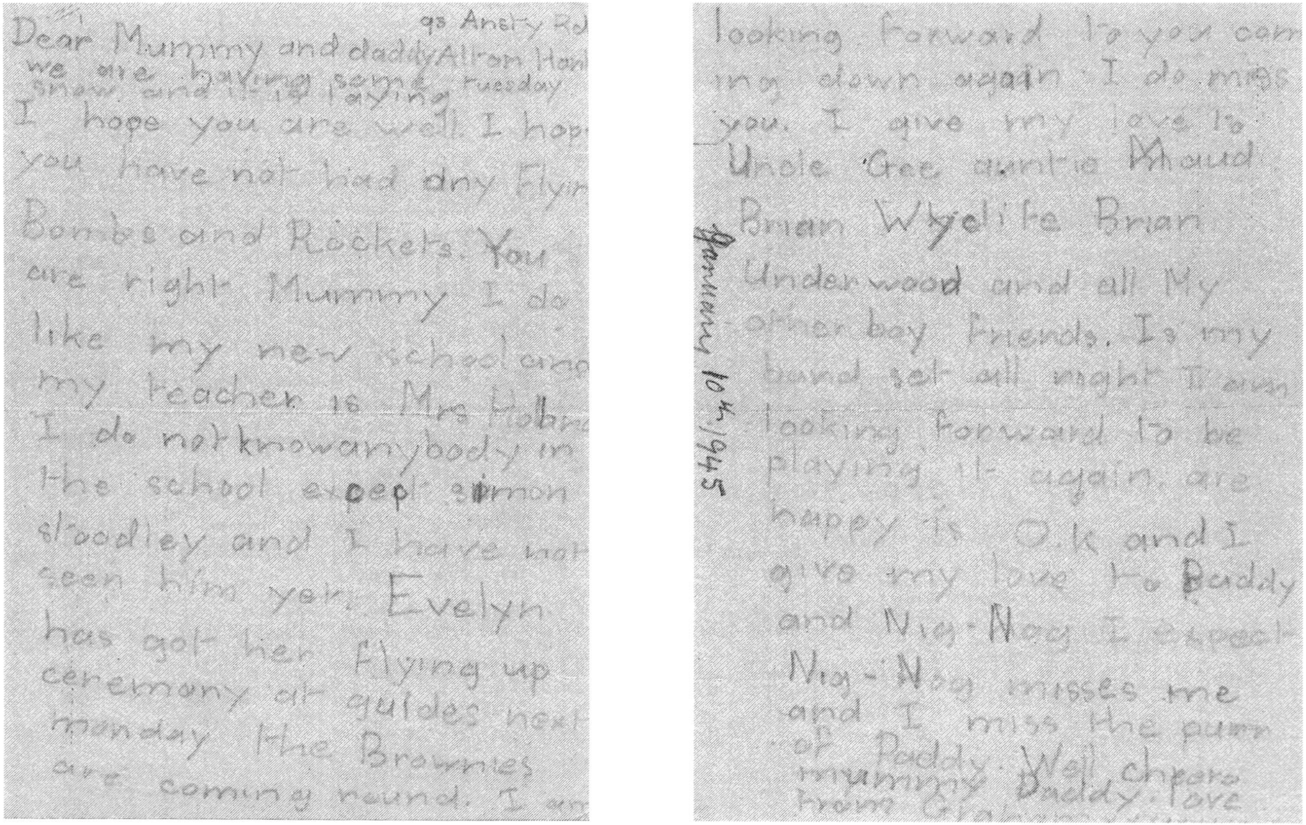

95 Anerly Rd

Dear Mummy and daddy Altom Hant
we are having some
snow and it is laying tuesday
I hope you are well I hope
you have not had any Flyin
Bombs and Rockets. You
are right Mummy I do
like my new school and
my teacher is Mrs Hobb
I do not know anybody in
the school except simon
shoodley and I have not
seen him yet. Evelyn
has got her flying up
ceremony at guides next
monday the Brownies
are coming round. I am
looking forward to you com
ing down again I do miss
you. I give my love to
Uncle Gee auntie Maud
Brian Wyclife Brian
Underwood and all My
other boy friends. Is my
band set all right I am
looking forward to be
playing it again, are
happy is O.k and I
give my love to Paddy
and Nig-Nog I expect
Nig-Nog misses me
and I miss the purr
of Paddy. Well cheero
mummy Daddy. love
from ...

January 10th 1945

Letter from my third stay at Thorn Cottage (January 1945)

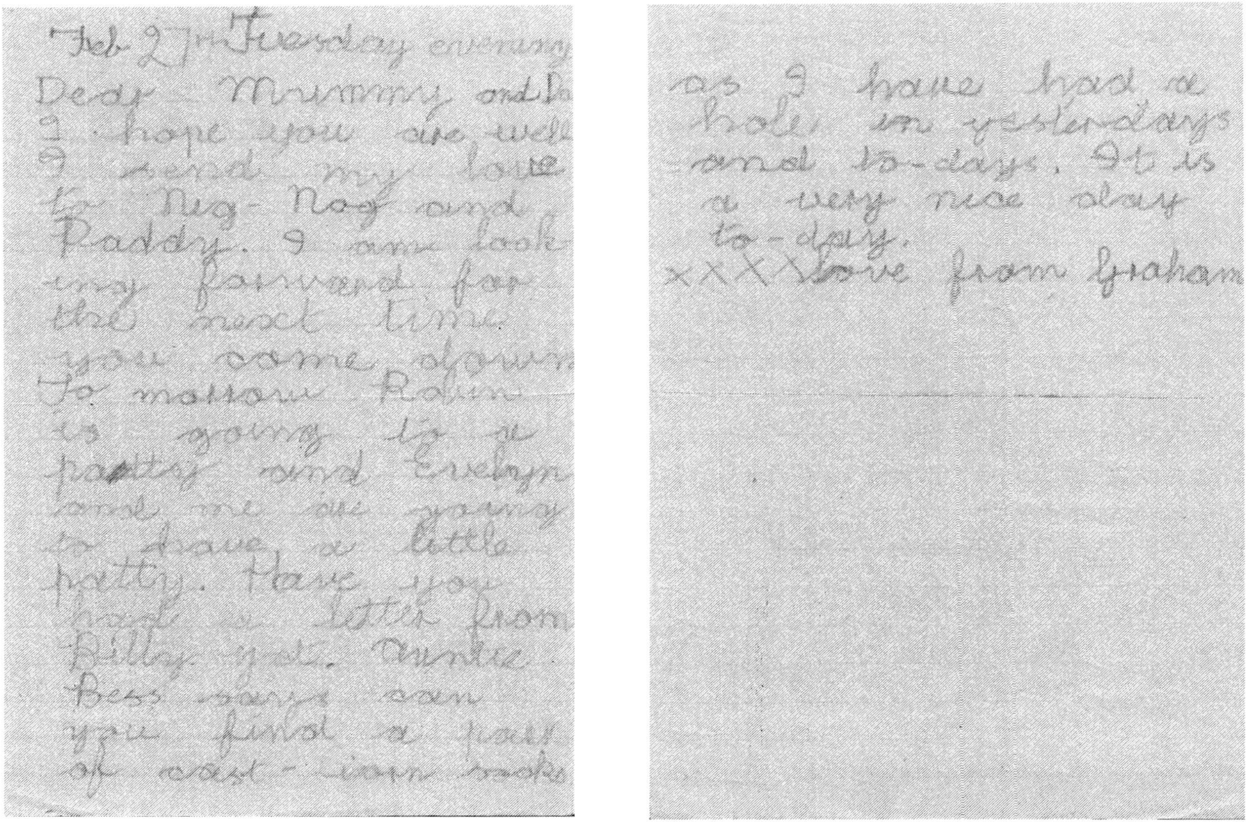

My first 'real writing' (February 1945)

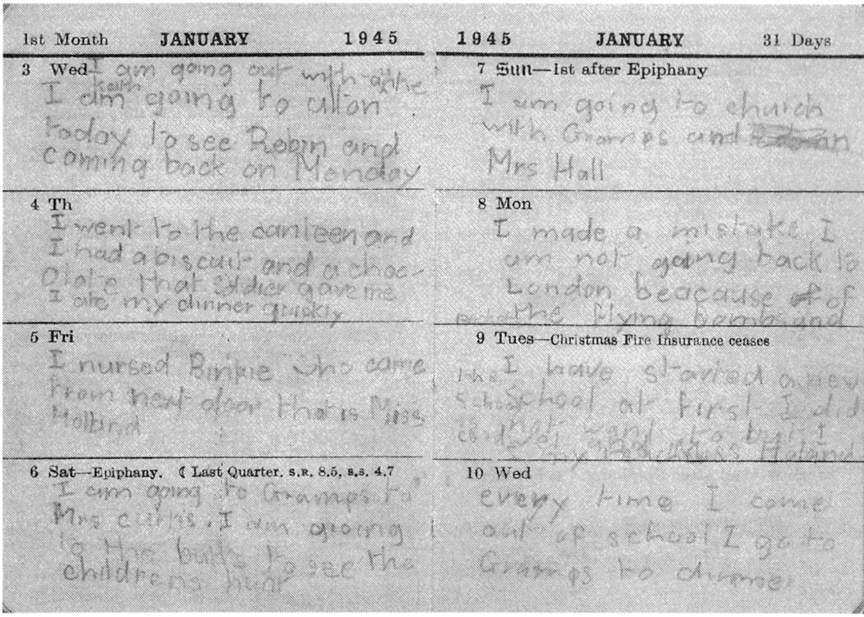
1st Month JANUARY 1945 | 1945 JANUARY 31 Days

3 Wed — I am going out with Anne I am going to [illegible] today to see Robin and coming back on Monday

4 Th — I went to the canteen and I had a biscuit and a chocolate that soldier gave me I ate my dinner quickly

5 Fri — I nursed Binkie she came from next door that is Miss Holland

6 Sat—Epiphany. ☾ Last Quarter. S.R. 8.5, S.S. 4.7 — I am going to Gramps to Mrs Curtis. I am going to the baths to see the childrens [illegible]

7 Sun—1st after Epiphany — I am going to church with Gramps and Mrs Hall

8 Mon — I made a mistake I am not going back to London beacause of the flying bombs and

9 Tues—Christmas Fire Insurance ceases — I have started a new school at first I did not want to but I [illegible] Miss Holland

10 Wed — every time I come out of school I go to Gramps to dinner

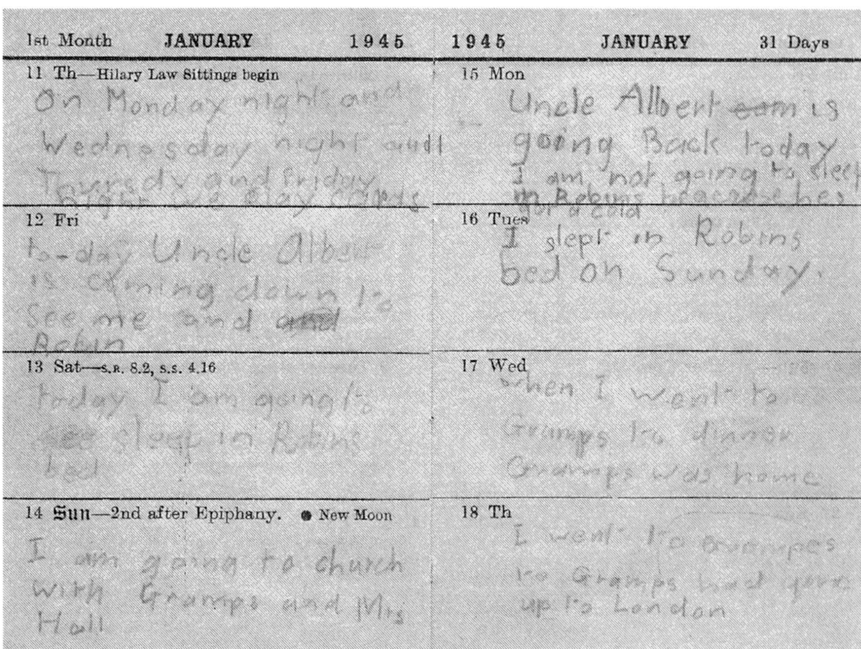
1st Month JANUARY 1945 | 1945 JANUARY 31 Days

11 Th—Hilary Law Sittings begin — On Monday night and Wednesday night and Thursday and Friday night we play cards

12 Fri — to-day Uncle Albert is coming down to see me and Robin

13 Sat—S.R. 8.2, S.S. 4.16 — today I am going to sleep in Robins bed

14 Sun—2nd after Epiphany. ● New Moon — I am going to church with Gramps and Mrs Hall

15 Mon — Uncle Albert is going Back today I am not going to sleep in Robins beacause he's got a cold

16 Tues — I slept in Robins bed on Sunday.

17 Wed — when I went to Gramps to dinner Gramps was home

18 Th — I went to Grampes to Gramps had gone up to London

My diary illustrates the uncertainties of wartime life

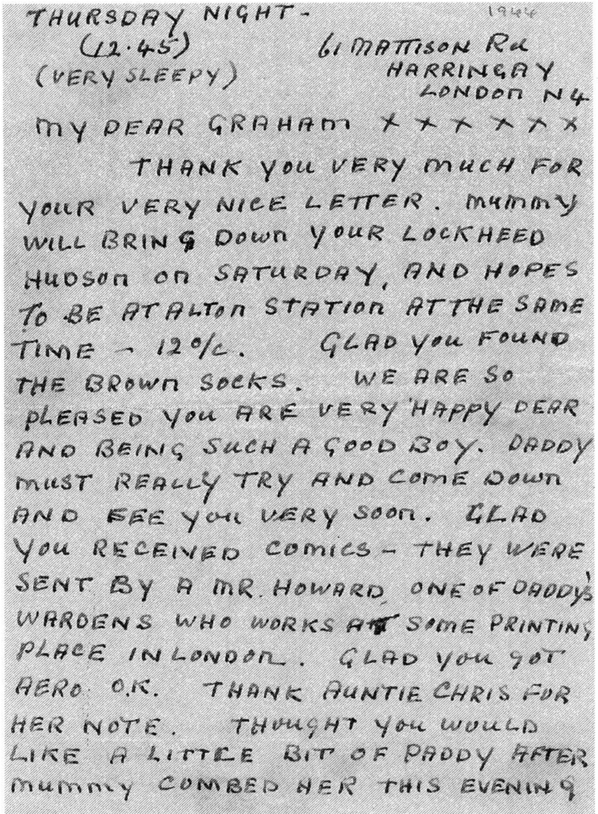
THURSDAY NIGHT - (12.45) (VERY SLEEPY)

1944

61 MATTISON Rd
HARRINGAY
LONDON N4

MY DEAR GRAHAM XXXXXX

THANK YOU VERY MUCH FOR YOUR VERY NICE LETTER. MUMMY WILL BRING DOWN YOUR LOCKHEED HUDSON ON SATURDAY, AND HOPES TO BE AT ALTON STATION AT THE SAME TIME - 12 o/c. GLAD YOU FOUND THE BROWN SOCKS. WE ARE SO PLEASED YOU ARE VERY HAPPY DEAR AND BEING SUCH A GOOD BOY. DADDY MUST REALLY TRY AND COME DOWN AND SEE YOU VERY SOON. GLAD YOU RECEIVED COMICS - THEY WERE SENT BY A MR. HOWARD, ONE OF DADDY'S WARDENS WHO WORKS AT SOME PRINTING PLACE IN LONDON. GLAD YOU GOT AERO O.K. THANK AUNTIE CHRIS FOR HER NOTE. THOUGHT YOU WOULD LIKE A LITTLE BIT OF PADDY AFTER MUMMY COMBED HER THIS EVENING

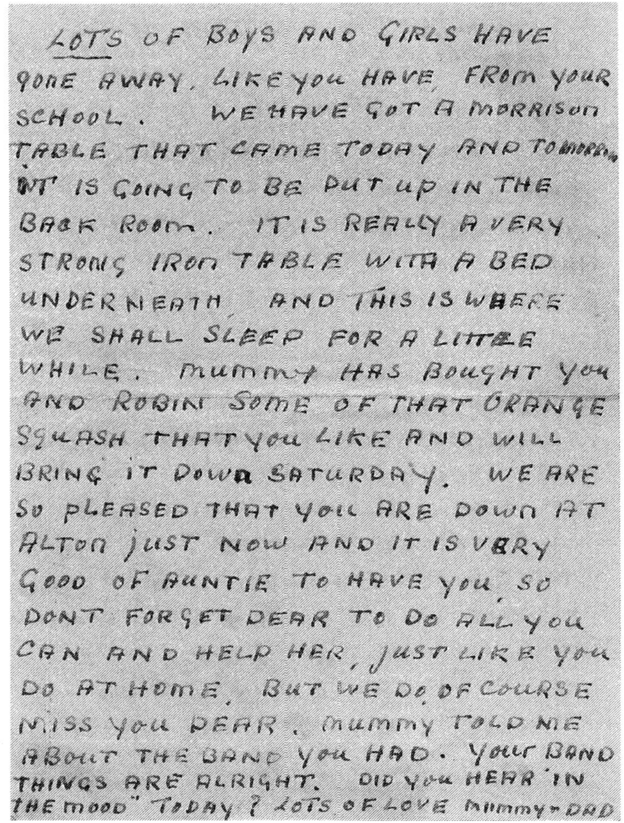
LOTS OF BOYS AND GIRLS HAVE GONE AWAY, LIKE YOU HAVE, FROM YOUR SCHOOL. WE HAVE GOT A MORRISON TABLE THAT CAME TODAY AND TOMORROW IT IS GOING TO BE PUT UP IN THE BACK ROOM. IT IS REALLY A VERY STRONG IRON TABLE WITH A BED UNDERNEATH AND THIS IS WHERE WE SHALL SLEEP FOR A LITTLE WHILE. MUMMY HAS BOUGHT YOU AND ROBIN SOME OF THAT ORANGE SQUASH THAT YOU LIKE AND WILL BRING IT DOWN SATURDAY. WE ARE SO PLEASED THAT YOU ARE DOWN AT ALTON JUST NOW AND IT IS VERY GOOD OF AUNTIE TO HAVE YOU, SO DONT FORGET DEAR TO DO ALL YOU CAN AND HELP HER, JUST LIKE YOU DO AT HOME, BUT WE DO OF COURSE MISS YOU DEAR. MUMMY TOLD ME ABOUT THE BAND YOU HAD. YOUR BAND THINGS ARE ALRIGHT. DID YOU HEAR "IN THE MOOD" TODAY? LOTS OF LOVE MUMMY + DAD

Letter from my father (late June /early July 1944)

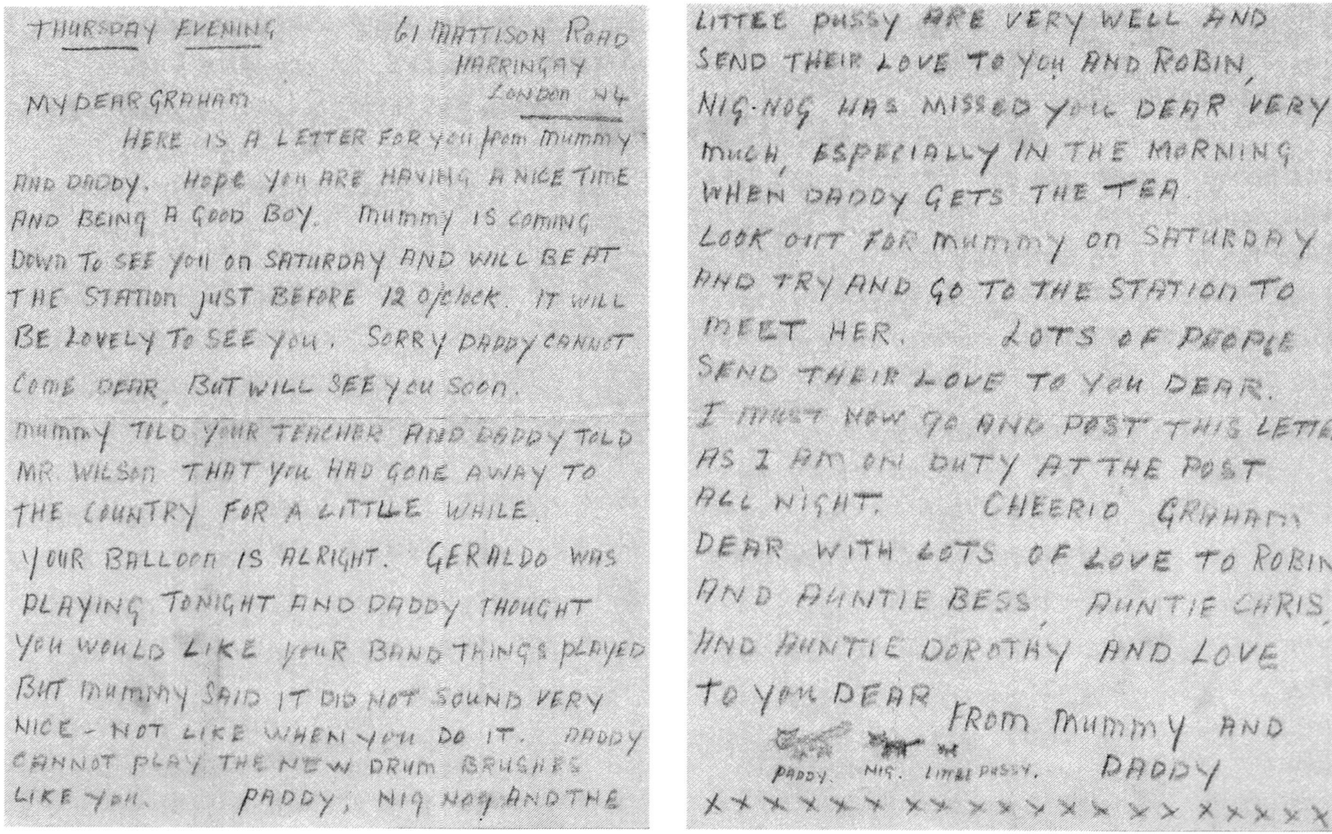

THURSDAY EVENING

61 MATTISON ROAD
HARRINGAY
LONDON N4

MY DEAR GRAHAM

HERE IS A LETTER FOR YOU FROM MUMMY AND DADDY. HOPE YOU ARE HAVING A NICE TIME AND BEING A GOOD BOY. MUMMY IS COMING DOWN TO SEE YOU ON SATURDAY AND WILL BE AT THE STATION JUST BEFORE 12 O/CLOCK. IT WILL BE LOVELY TO SEE YOU. SORRY DADDY CANNOT COME DEAR, BUT WILL SEE YOU SOON.

MUMMY TOLD YOUR TEACHER AND DADDY TOLD MR WILSON THAT YOU HAD GONE AWAY TO THE COUNTRY FOR A LITTLE WHILE.

YOUR BALLOON IS ALRIGHT. GERALDO WAS PLAYING TONIGHT AND DADDY THOUGHT YOU WOULD LIKE YOUR BAND THINGS PLAYED BUT MUMMY SAID IT DID NOT SOUND VERY NICE - NOT LIKE WHEN YOU DO IT. DADDY CANNOT PLAY THE NEW DRUM BRUSHES LIKE YOU. PADDY, NIG NOG AND THE LITTLE PUSSY ARE VERY WELL AND SEND THEIR LOVE TO YOU AND ROBIN, NIG-NOG HAS MISSED YOU DEAR VERY MUCH, ESPECIALLY IN THE MORNING WHEN DADDY GETS THE TEA.

LOOK OUT FOR MUMMY ON SATURDAY AND TRY AND GO TO THE STATION TO MEET HER. LOTS OF PEOPLE SEND THEIR LOVE TO YOU DEAR.

I MUST NOW GO AND POST THIS LETTER AS I AM ON DUTY AT THE POST ALL NIGHT. CHEERIO GRAHAM DEAR WITH LOTS OF LOVE TO ROBIN AND AUNTIE BESS, AUNTIE CHRIS, AND AUNTIE DOROTHY AND LOVE TO YOU DEAR

FROM MUMMY AND DADDY

XXXXXXXXXXXXXXXXXXX

Letter from my father (January 1945)

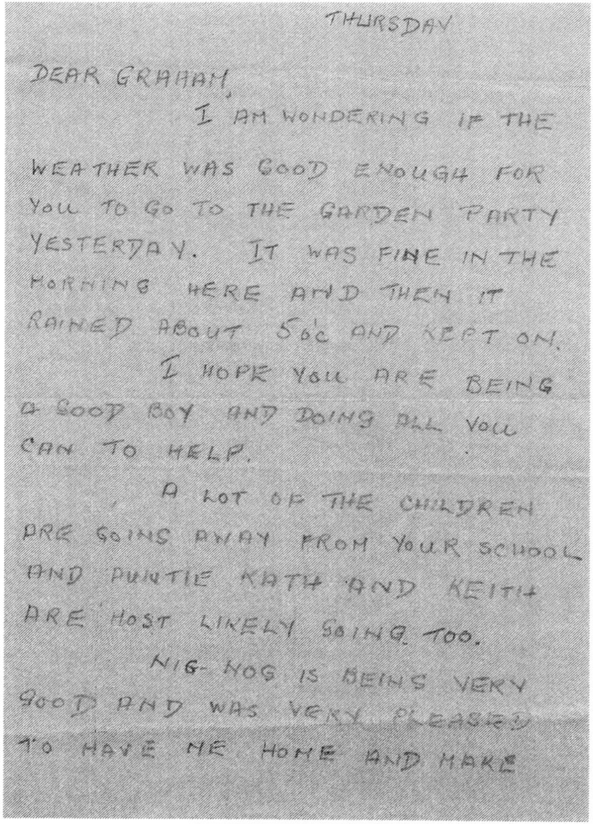

THURSDAY

DEAR GRAHAM,

I AM WONDERING IF THE WEATHER WAS GOOD ENOUGH FOR YOU TO GO TO THE GARDEN PARTY YESTERDAY. IT WAS FINE IN THE MORNING HERE AND THEN IT RAINED ABOUT 5 O'C AND KEPT ON.

I HOPE YOU ARE BEING A GOOD BOY AND DOING ALL YOU CAN TO HELP.

A LOT OF THE CHILDREN ARE GOING AWAY FROM YOUR SCHOOL AND AUNTIE KATH AND KEITH ARE MOST LIKELY GOING TOO.

NIG-NOG IS BEING VERY GOOD AND WAS VERY PLEASED TO HAVE ME HOME AND MAKE

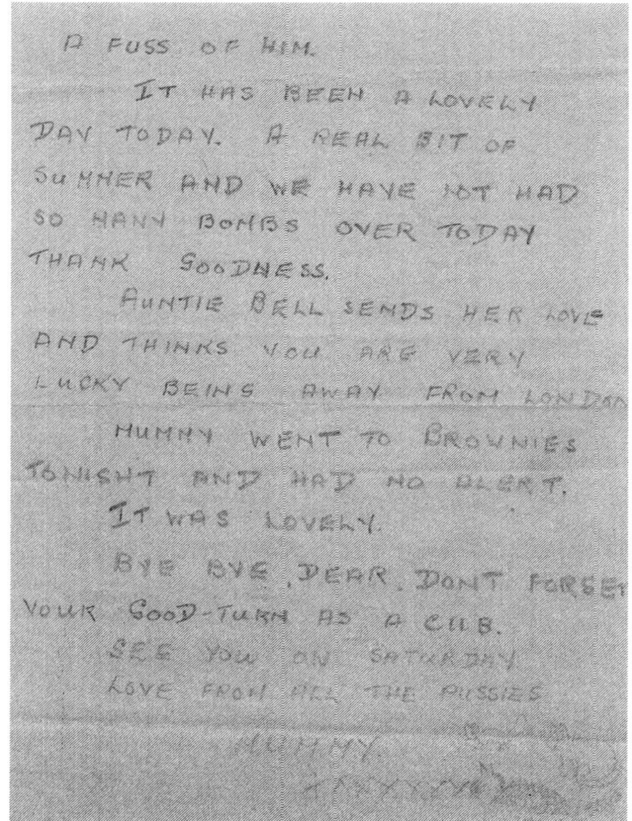

A FUSS OF HIM.

IT HAS BEEN A LOVELY DAY TODAY. A REAL BIT OF SUMMER AND WE HAVE NOT HAD SO MANY BOMBS OVER TODAY THANK GOODNESS.

AUNTIE BELL SENDS HER LOVE AND THINKS YOU ARE VERY LUCKY BEING AWAY FROM LONDON.

MUMMY WENT TO BROWNIES TONIGHT AND HAD NO ALERT. IT WAS LOVELY.

BYE BYE, DEAR. DONT FORGET YOUR GOOD-TURN AS A CUB.

SEE YOU ON SATURDAY

LOVE FROM ALL THE PUSSIES

MUMMY.

Letter from my mother (probably August 1944)

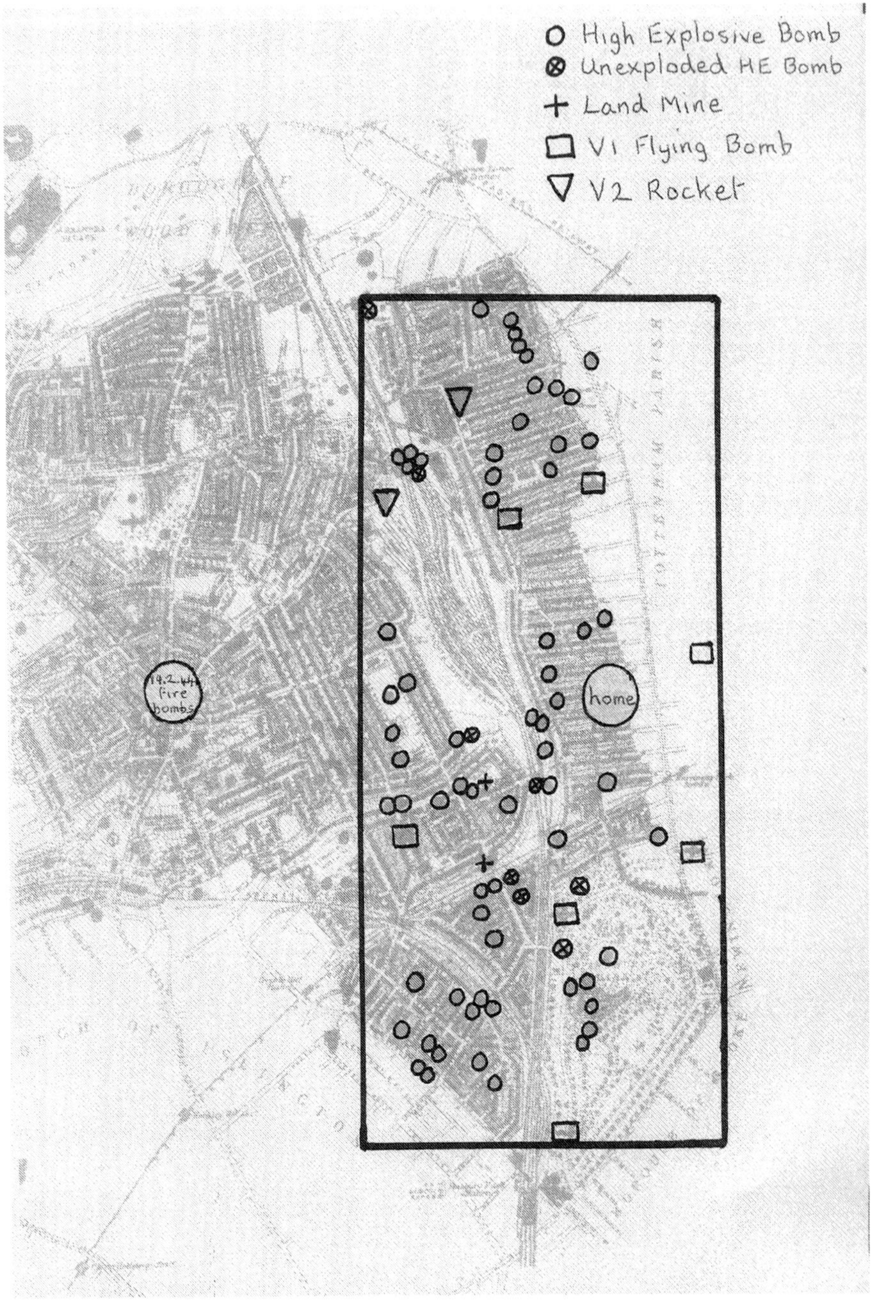

My home area, Harringay, North London, showing the 85 bomb incidents during World War II
(Map reproduced by kind permission of The Hornsey Historical Society)

The damage caused by the morning (8.15a.m.) V-2 rocket on 10th November 1944 that blew in our windows. 10 people were killed and 78 injured.
(Photograph courtesy of the Imperial War Musum, London - HU 609 31)

This is why I stayed in Alton for a further 3 months. On the 8th January 1945, about midday, a V-2 rocket destroyed 14 houses and badly damaged 70 killing 14 people and injuring 99.
(Photograph courtesy of Bruce Castle Museum - Haringey Libraries, Archives and Museum Service)

The ARP warden 'post' opposite our house (my father is centre foreground)

My cousin Bill in his flying gear

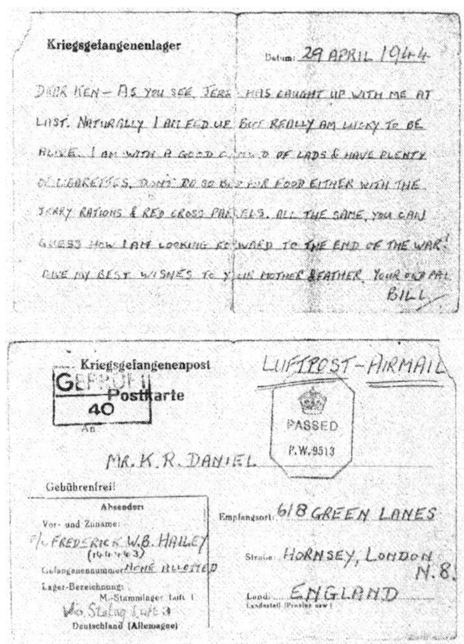

Kriegsgefangenenlager

Datum: 29 APRIL 1944

DEAR KEN – AS YOU SEE JERRY HAS CAUGHT UP WITH ME AT LAST. NATURALLY I AM FED UP BUT REALLY AM LUCKY TO BE ALIVE. I AM WITH A GOOD CROWD OF LADS & HAVE PLENTY OF CIGARETTES, DON'T DO SO BAD FOR FOOD EITHER WITH THE JERRY RATIONS & RED CROSS PARCELS. ALL THE SAME, YOU CAN GUESS HOW I AM LOOKING FORWARD TO THE END OF THE WAR! GIVE MY BEST WISHES TO YOUR MOTHER & FATHER. YOUR OLD PAL

BILL.

Kriegsgefangenenpost

GEPRÜFT 40

Postkarte

LUFTPOST-AIRMAIL

PASSED P.W. 9513

An MR. K.R. DANIEL

Gebührenfrei!

Absender:
Vor- und Zuname: F/L FREDERICK W.B. HAILEY (144443)
Gefangenennummer: NONE ALLOTTED
Lager-Bezeichnung: M.-Stammlager Luft 1
Via Stalag Luft 3
Deutschland (Allemagne)

Empfangsort: 618 GREEN LANES
Straße: HORNSEY, LONDON N.8
Land: ENGLAND
Landesteil (Provinz usw.)

When my cousin Bill was a Prisoner of War in Germany he sent this letter to his friend Ken

Our street VE Day party (I am central, wearing a crown and a tie)

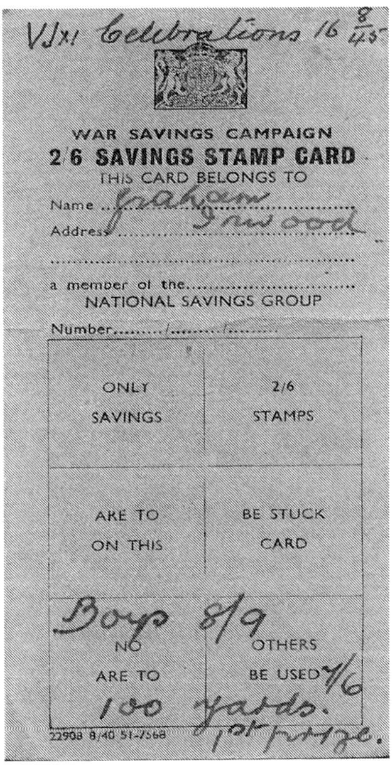

VJx! Celebrations 16 8/45

WAR SAVINGS CAMPAIGN

2/6 SAVINGS STAMP CARD

THIS CARD BELONGS TO

Name Graham

Address Inwood

a member of the ....

NATIONAL SAVINGS GROUP

Number ..../......./.......

ONLY 2/6 SAVINGS STAMPS ARE TO BE STUCK ON THIS CARD

Boys 8/9

NO OTHERS ARE TO BE USED 4/6

100 yards.

1st prize.

22908 8/40 51-7568

My prize for winning the 100 yards sprint at Salcombe, Devon, on VJ Day

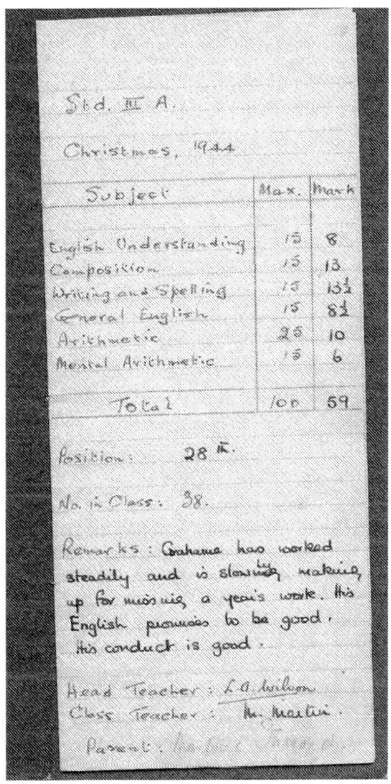

Std. III A.

Christmas, 1944

Subject	Max.	Mark
English Understanding	15	8
Composition	15	13
Writing and Spelling	15	13½
General English	15	8½
Arithmetic	25	10
Mental Arithmetic	15	6
Total	100	59

Position: 28th.

No. in Class: 38.

Remarks: Graham has worked steadily and is slowly making up for missing a year's work. His English promises to be good. His conduct is good.

Head Teacher: L.A. Wilson

Class Teacher: M. Martin.

Parent: [illegible]

My school report from my London Junior School for Christmas 1944

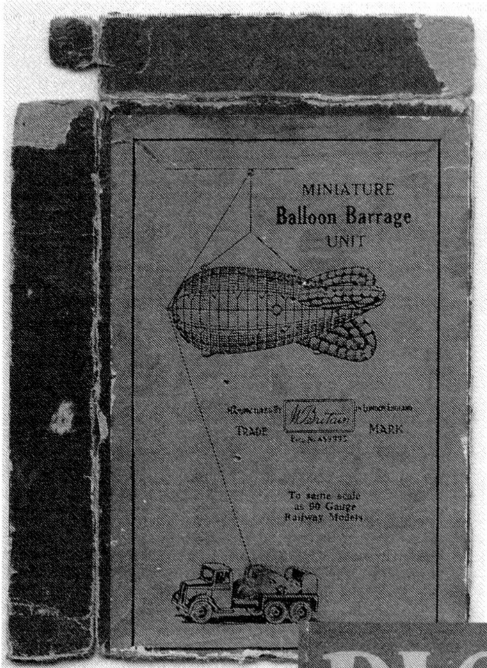

Left: The box label of my toy barrage balloon

Below: My favourite story book about a barrage balloon which captured a German fighter plane and its pilot

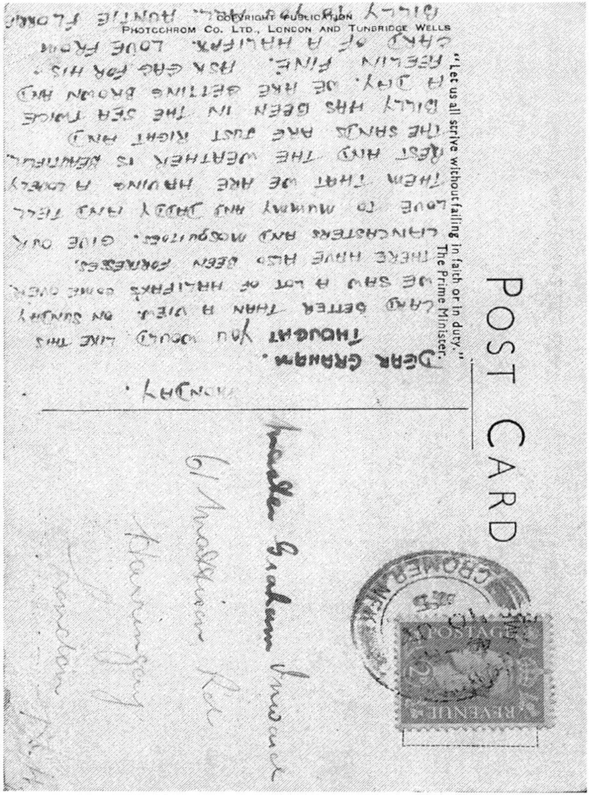

My cousin Bill arrived back from the German POW camp in mid-May 1945. In July he went on holiday with his mother (Aunty Florrie) who sent me this card showing a Halifax bomber

The advertisement for the Evacuees exhibition at the Imperial War Museum
(Reproduced by kind permission of The Imperial War Museum, London)

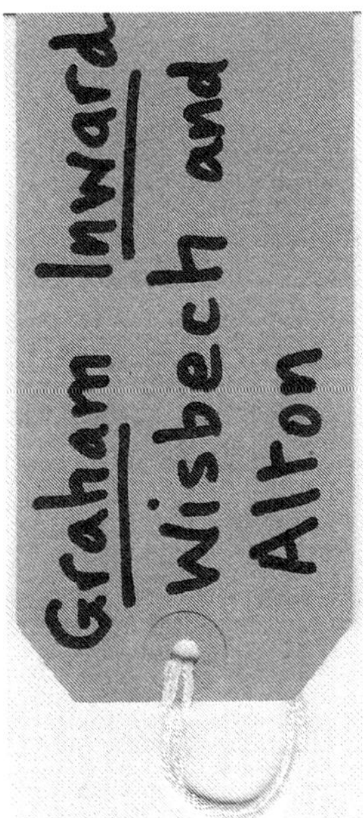

The label I wore at the Evacuees exhibition

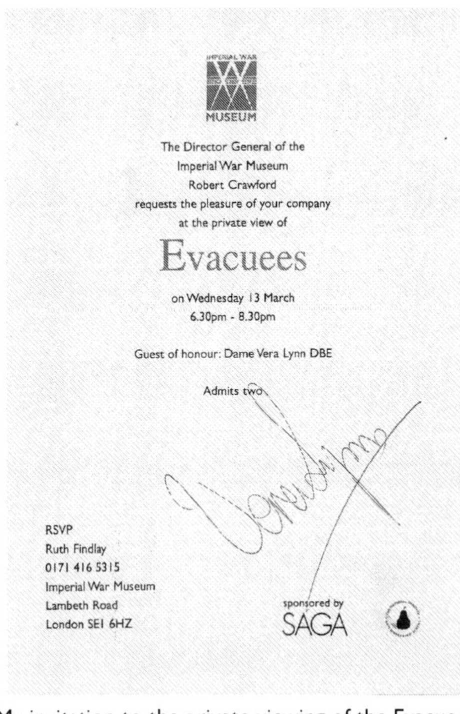

My invitation to the private viewing of the Evacuees exhibition with Dame Vera Lynn's signature

Displays including my toy aircraft and buses and my books and toys

My sheet music of 'Goodnight Children Everywhere' displayed next to Dame Vera Lynn's master record of the song. My grandson Jordan looks on

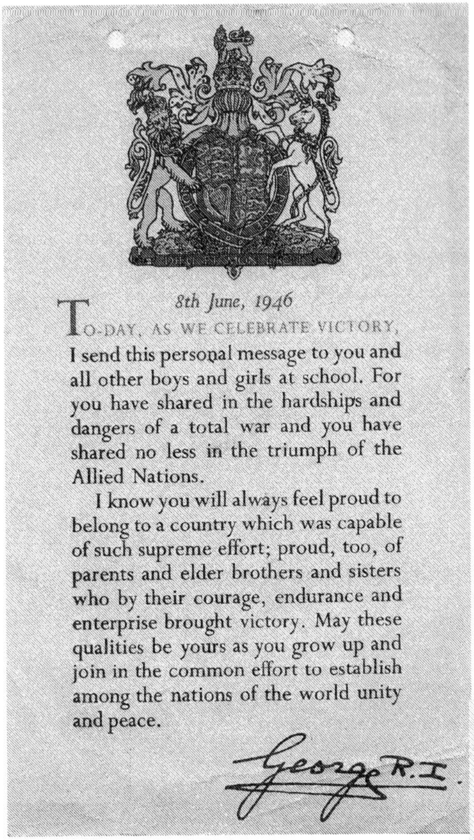

8th June, 1946

TO-DAY, AS WE CELEBRATE VICTORY, I send this personal message to you and all other boys and girls at school. For you have shared in the hardships and dangers of a total war and you have shared no less in the triumph of the Allied Nations.

I know you will always feel proud to belong to a country which was capable of such supreme effort; proud, too, of parents and elder brothers and sisters who by their courage, endurance and enterprise brought victory. May these qualities be yours as you grow up and join in the common effort to establish among the nations of the world unity and peace.

George R.I.

Above: All school pupils received this celebration certificate in June 1946

Right: My father and I (1954)